MASTER THE ART OF STORYTELLING TO SELL LIKE CRAZY

A Book on Mastering the Art of Persuasion through Story Selling Method

James Edwards

TABLE OF CONTENTS

INTRODUCTION

The capacity to fascinate an audience with captivating stories is an invaluable skill in the ever-changing world of business and marketing. Stories possess the ability to strike a chord, motivate, and spur action. This book takes you on a journey to discover the techniques for becoming an expert storyteller and how you can use them to boost your sales.

The craft of storytelling appears as a powerful tool to cut through the clutter and establish a deep connection with your audience in a market that is overflowing with options and information. Whether you're a business owner, a sales expert, or a marketing enthusiast, the ideas presented in these pages will enable you to create compelling stories that captivate readers and leave a lasting impression.

We'll examine the psychological foundations that underlie the power of stories as we delve into their complexities. You'll learn how to craft stories that arouse feelings in your audience, foster a sense of trust, and ultimately motivate them to act. Each chapter aims to provide you with the knowledge and skills necessary to improve your storytelling abilities, from identifying your target audience to developing an engaging story twist.

The trip ahead looks to be instructive as well as useful, with plenty of tactics that you can easily implement. By the time you finish reading this book, you will not only understand the craft of storytelling but also know how to strategically use it in your sales efforts to change the way you go about things and accomplish exceptional results.

Prepare yourself for a life-changing journey as we reveal the techniques that will help you 'Master the Art of Storytelling to Sell Like Crazy.' The path to becoming a skilled storyteller begins right now.

CHAPTER ONE

The Power of Storytelling on Sales

A highly influential skill in the fast-paced world of sales is the capacity to enrapture an audience and forge a lasting connection in an environment where goods and services strive for consumers' attention. Not only is storytelling an effective tool for authors and performers, but it's also a powerful tool for salespeople. This chapter examines the importance of storytelling in sales, highlighting the transformational potential of gripping tales.

The Story's Scientific Basis

The human brain is uniquely engaged by stories. According to neurological research, when we hear an engaging story, our brains release the hormone oxytocin, which is linked to empathy and trust. The audience becomes more open to the message being delivered as a result of this chemical reaction that forges a bond between the storyteller and the audience.

Establishing a connection and promoting trust is critical in the sales process. Salespeople can strengthen their persuasiveness by building an emotional connection with potential customers by applying the science of storytelling.

The Problem of Remembering Messages

Customers find it difficult to recall particular attributes of the product or technical information in an ocean of information overload. But stories stick in people's memories. A persuasive story enables the salesman to incorporate important points into a memorable and relatable story. This improves the information's palatable quality and raises the likelihood that it will be remembered long after the sales presentation is over.

Overcoming Objections with Storytelling

Consumers frequently have reservations or worries when thinking about making a purchase. Sophisticated storytellers use stories to address these objections rather than barging them with numbers. The salesperson can successfully allay doubts and promote confidence in the good or service by crafting a narrative that reflects the customer's circumstances and shows how others overcome comparable obstacles.

Creating Emotional Coherence

Individuals use logic to justify their emotional-driven decisions after making them. Salespeople can access the emotional side of decision-making by using storytelling. A salesperson can make an impression that lasts longer than a simple transaction by telling tales that arouse particular feelings, such as joy, fear, or aspiration.

The Influence of Captivating Stories

A captivating story transports the audience to a world in which they can see themselves, going beyond a straightforward retelling of events. This immersive experience affects perception in addition to grabbing attention. A captivating story enables the audience to visualize themselves profiting in a practical way from the good or service rather than overwhelming them with a list of features.

Case Studies as Influential Narratives

In essence, case studies are success stories. They provide examples of how a good or service improved a customer's life or company. A well-written case study gives prospective clients a concrete example of the value they can anticipate by turning data and facts into a compelling story.

Finally, storytelling proves to be a potent weapon in the cutthroat world of sales, where there is a strong need to be unique. Salespeople can establish a stronger emotional connection, overcome objections, and increase information recall when they use it to engage their audience on a deeper level. It is important to recognize the impact that persuasive stories have in converting prospective customers into happy patrons and devoted supporters.

CHAPTER TWO

The Basis of a Persuasive Story

Any effective communication strategy starts with a well-crafted story. Knowing the fundamentals of persuasive storytelling is essential whether you're a company trying to sell a product, a non-profit looking for funding for a cause, or an individual trying to make a strong argument. We'll explore the fundamental elements of a compelling story in this chapter, which include knowing your audience, establishing your brand's story, and developing a unique selling proposition (USP).

Recognizing Your Target Audience

To write a compelling story, you must first identify your target audience. Your message might be ignored if you don't know exactly who you are attempting to persuade. Take into account your target audience's psychographics, behaviors, and demographics. What are their wants, needs, and areas of discomfort? What spurs them into action?

These Three Elements Will Help You Understand Your Audience

1. Audience Demographics: Determine the fundamental attributes of your audience, including age, gender, location, and income. You can use this information to better craft a message that speaks to their unique situation.

2. Psychographics of your Audience: Learn more about your audience's mentality. Recognize their lifestyles, interests, values, and beliefs. You'll be able to establish a more intimate and emotional connection with them if you have a perfect understanding of this information.

3. Audience Behavior: Examine the acts and demeanor of your audience. What routines do they follow? How do they gather knowledge? Understanding how your audience engages with the environment will direct your storytelling strategy.

You will be prepared to write a story that specifically addresses the needs and goals of your intended audience by developing thorough audience personas based on these factors.

Setting Your Brand's Narrative

The narrative that captures the core of your identity is called your brand story. It explores your brand's distinctive values, mission, and personality in addition to the goods and services you provide. Establishing an emotional connection with your audience through a compelling brand story cultivates trust and loyalty.

These Three Elements Are Essential to Developing Your Brand Story

1. Origins and Values: Tell the tale of how your company's brand was founded. Emphasize the values that guide your company and coincide with those of your target audience. In order to establish a deep connection, authenticity is essential.

2. Relatability: By adding components that connect with the experiences of your audience, you can make your brand relatable. Putting common struggles, accomplishments, or goals on display makes your brand seem more relatable.

3. Consistency: Make sure that every touchpoint has consistency. Your overall brand identity, messaging, and visuals should all tell the same story about your brand. Maintaining consistency improves brand recall and strengthens the narrative.

Developing a USP (Unique Selling Proposition)

Your product, service, or idea's unique selling proposition (USP) is what makes it stand out from the competition. That's the thing that makes your audience pick you out of the competition. A captivating USP makes it clear what value you offer and gives your audience a reason to act.

These Three Elements Are Important to Consider When Creating a USP

1. Determine Your Strengths: Consider your advantages in terms of quality, creativity, economy, or top-notch customer service. Making use of these advantages should be your USP.

2. Solve a Problem: Deal with a particular issue or source of discomfort for your audience. Your offering should offer a better or distinct solution than competing products on the market.

3. Communicate Clearly: Clearly state your USP in a succinct and understandable message. Skip the jargon and concentrate on using language that makes sense to your audience. Your USP ought to be simple to comprehend and recall.

In conclusion, developing a captivating USP, defining your brand story, and knowing your audience are the cornerstones of a persuasive story. Focusing on these components will help you tell a story that enthralls your audience, earns their trust, and inspires them to act.

CHAPTER THREE

How to Write a Compelling Story

Capturing an audience is an essential skill in the narrative domain, be it business or literary. A compelling story may captivate readers, make an impact, and deliver your point clearly. We will examine the essential components of an engaging story in this chapter, emphasizing character growth, storyline and organization, business setting, and the use of conflict to increase reader involvement.

Character Formation:

Any story's core is its cast of characters. Well-developed characters help to connect the audience, whether they are real people in a business narrative or imaginary personas in a novel. Your "characters" in the business world could be your clients, colleagues, or even the organization. Make sure your characters have distinct objectives, are relatable, and go through significant development if you want your story to be compelling. Permit your audience to comprehend their struggles, accomplishments, and current path.

Storyline and Organization:

A compelling story is built on a solid plot. In the business realm, your story may center on the difficulties your organization encountered, the tactics you used, and the resultant success. Just as crucial is how your story is organized. Think about using a three-act framework, in which the characters and scene are introduced, the conflict or obstacles are presented, and the problems are satisfactorily resolved at the end. This arrangement preserves equilibrium and keeps your audience interested all the way through.

Creating the Scene:

A backdrop is necessary for your company tale, just as it is for a novel. Give a detailed account of your working environment that puts the events that take place in context. Assist your audience in seeing the difficulties and victories that exist within the particular context of your sector. A rich narrative is enhanced by a well-established setting, regardless of the reason behind the changes in consumer tastes, technical breakthroughs, or competitive market conditions.

Including Conflict to Encourage Engagement:

Every story needs conflict to move forward. Conflict in the business sector can take many different forms, such as rivalry inside the company, internal strife, or conquering roadblocks en route to achievement. Drawing attention to these conflicts helps your audience relate to the journey while also generating excitement. Be open and honest about the difficulties that your characters — employees, bosses, or the business itself — have faced, and show how they overcame them.

Finally, an engaging story comprises engrossing character growth, a meticulously crafted storyline, a compelling corporate setting, and audience-resonant tensions. Combining these components will allow you to tell a story that engages, inspires, and informs. Learning the craft of storytelling is a vital tool for successful communication in the business world, whether you're discussing a business's past, a success story, or a vision for the future.

CHAPTER FOUR

Cultivating Emotional Connection

Human interactions, decisions, and experiences are greatly influenced by emotions. In order to establish intuitive bonds, one must first recognize and utilize these deep facets of human nature. Emotions are diverse and universal; they include but are not limited to, happiness, sorrow, fear, rage, surprise, and disgust.

Three Aspects of Human Nature for Cultivating Emotional Connections

1. Emotional Intelligence: Establishing deep connections requires the development of emotional intelligence. This entails being sensitive to other people's feelings in addition to being aware of and comprehending your own. Empathy and active listening are two ways that people can connect with others more deeply.

2. Authenticity and Vulnerability: These are essential components for evoking feelings. Sincere emotions and experiences are shared, which promotes an atmosphere of openness and trust. Vulnerability-displaying leaders foster connection and loyalty within their teams.

3. Empathy in Communication: Empathy is a necessary component of effective communication; words alone are not enough. Talks can be more meaningful and productive when both parties are aware of each other's perspectives and feelings. Empathy establishes the groundwork for robust emotional bonds in both personal and professional contexts.

Crafting Engaging Experiences

Creating experiences that speak to people's innermost feelings is a necessary step in developing emotional bonds. This calls for a deliberate strategy that takes into account common values, goals, and difficulties.

Three Methods to Craft Engaging Experiences to Promote Emotional Bonds

1. Storytelling as a Tool: Since the beginning of time, people have told stories. Stories are a powerful tool for fostering connections because they have the ability to arouse feelings. Storytelling makes events relevant and memorable, whether it's in leadership, marketing, or casual chats.

2. Shared Beliefs and Values: Highlighting and identifying common values and beliefs promotes a feeling of togetherness and belonging. People are drawn to others who share their values, which lays the groundwork for a deep emotional connection. This idea holds true for ties made outside of organizations as well as within them.

3. Inclusive Experiences: Developing inclusive experiences guarantees a sense of belonging for people with different origins and viewpoints. Emotional relationships are strengthened when people feel seen and appreciated. A culture where people value and appreciate one another's feelings and experiences is promoted by inclusion.

The Study of Emotional Resonance Psychology

In order to establish long-lasting relationships, it is crucial to comprehend the psychology underlying emotional resonance. This entails identifying the elements that contribute to the emotional effect of particular situations, messages, or people.

Three Emotional Resonance Factors to Consider When Creating Emotional Bonds

1. Mirror Neurons and Human Connection: Mirror neurons are essential for human communication. Mirror neurons may fire when people notice emotions in others, resulting in a shared emotional experience. This phenomenon supports the theory that feelings are transmissible and serve as the foundation for empathy.

2. Positive Reinforcement: Emotions and positive experiences strengthen bonds. Positive reinforcement fortifies emotional ties, whether it comes from praise, acknowledgment, or mutual accomplishments. Positive reinforcement is a powerful tool that leaders and organizations may use to create a positive and encouraging atmosphere.

3. The Power of Nostalgia: Evoking strong emotions is one of nostalgia's special talents. Drawing from the past can evoke intense feelings, whether through reliving shared memories or adding nostalgic details to new situations. This is a powerful tool for relationship-building, marketing, and storytelling.

In conclusion, developing emotional ties requires a blend of comparable experiences, emotional intelligence, and knowledge of the psychological elements that influence emotional resonance. Through the adoption of genuineness, compassion, and the potency of mutual feelings, people and institutions can establish relationships that endure over time.

CHAPTER FIVE

Four Techniques to Perfecting in Storytelling

1. The Art of Pictorial Expression

The brushstroke that conjures up vivid images in your readers' thoughts is pictorial expression. Their senses are stimulated, bringing the narrative to life. Engage your audience by drawing them into the world you've created, rather than just delivering data. To arouse feelings and establish a deeper connection with your readers, use sensory details.

For example, instead of writing "It was a cold night," explain the feeling of cold that permeates the atmosphere, the frost that clings to everything, and the way the moonlight turns breath into mist. By employing evocative language, you enable your readers to engage with your story on a visceral level and are drawn right into the action.

2. Exhibit rather than Explain

The proverbial "show, don't tell" still holds true and is essential to good storytelling. Show feelings and events through actions, speech, and sensory nuances rather than stating them outright. Let readers come to their own conclusions and enjoy the story as it unfolds.

For example, portray a character's clenched fists, the red glow that began to appear on their necks, or the piercing tone of their voice instead of stating that they are angry. This method encourages readers to establish a closer connection with the people and events while also actively engaging them.

3. Employing Metaphors and Analogies

Metaphors and analogies are effective tools for explaining difficult concepts or feelings by making connections to ideas that are easier to understand. They give your narrative more depth and nuance and give readers a different viewpoint. Make an effort to use analogies that your audience can relate to in order to help them understand the unexpected.

Saying something like "a climb up a steep, winding mountain" to describe a difficult journey, for example, instantly invokes thoughts of hardship, determination, and the ultimate reward at the summit. The reader's experience is enhanced when analogies and metaphors build a bridge between the familiar and the unknown.

4. Follow the Acronym 'KISS' in Writing Stories

The acronym KISS is an abbreviation for Keep It Simple Stupid. Though complex writing has its place, there is power in simplicity that is often overlooked. Simple, uncomplicated language makes the story easier to understand and flows naturally. Aim for simplicity without compromising depth; avoid needless complexity by letting the plot develop organically.

Take the following instance: "The sun dipped below the horizon, casting a warm glow across the meadow" instead of "The radiant orb of the day descended, bathing the verdant expanse in a golden hue." Both communicate the same fundamental notion, but the former builds a deeper rapport with the reader by being easier to understand and more direct.

Finally, learning how to tell a story well requires a careful tango with the use of pictorial expression, the skill of demonstrating, the use of metaphors and analogies, and the strength of simplicity. You may create an engaging and immersive experience for your audience by including these aspects in your story fabric. Try out different combinations of these strategies to see which one best suits your own narrative style.

CHAPTER SIX

Harnessing the Skill of Storytelling Across Different Platforms

Storytelling has become more versatile in the modern period, spanning multiple channels and enabling storylines to reach a wide range of audiences. The ever-changing landscape of social media and the succinct and powerful elevator pitch have made the art of storytelling an essential communication skill. This chapter looks at the various ways that storytelling may be used, such as creating effective elevator pitches, using storytelling on social media, incorporating stories into presentations, and using storytelling in written content.

These Are Four Ways to Utilize Your Storytelling Skill

1. Developing an Effective Elevator Pitch

In the length of time required to use an elevator, an elevator pitch is a succinct and persuasive overview of a concept, initiative, or product. The key to creating a compelling elevator pitch is condensing the main points of your narrative into a succinct but memorable statement. To begin, decide what your main point is, draw attention to the issue or opportunity, and highlight the special features that make your story stand out. To create a lasting impression, use expressive words and evoke strong feelings. Recall that when giving an elevator pitch, conciseness and clarity are essential.

2. Using Social Media to Tell Stories

Social media platforms have developed into potent storytelling tools that offer chances to establish a personal connection with consumers. Adapt your narrative to the special qualities of each site, such as the visual appeal of Instagram, the succinctness of Twitter, or the formal tone of LinkedIn. To improve your story, use multimedia components like pictures, videos, and interactive elements. Use conversational media, engaging information, and real-time updates to interact with your audience. Storytelling on social media should be genuine, dependable, and in line with the identity of your company.

3. Including Narrative in Presentations

Presentations that are effective go beyond facts and figures to create a captivating story that draws in the audience. Start with a strong introduction that draws the reader in and establishes the mood. Tell a tale with a distinct beginning, middle, and end in your presentation. Make difficult material understandable by using engaging examples, metaphors, and anecdotes. Engage the audience with interactive features, talks, and questions. A compelling story improves recall and encourages a closer bond with your content.

4. Using Storytelling to Strengthen Written Content

Storytelling strategies are highly beneficial for written content, be it blog posts, essays, or reports. Start with an attention-grabbing headline that arouses readers' interest. Create a narrative twist to lead readers through the information and make it interesting and memorable. To give your work more depth, use conflict resolution, character development, and pictorial expression. Strike a balance between content and emotion so that readers can relate to you personally. A dull subject can become an engaging read with the right tale.

Finally, storytelling is a flexible technique that can be tailored to different media for optimal effect. The fundamentals of storytelling apply whether you're writing for an audience, making a brief elevator pitch, interacting on social media, or speaking to one. You may effectively express your message across several platforms and create a lasting imprint in the minds and hearts of your audience by knowing who your audience is, being real, and crafting compelling storylines.

CHAPTER SEVEN

Three Common Challenges of Storytelling and How to Overcome Them

1. Objections and Skepticism

Although stories are effective means of communication, they are not impervious to criticism and challenges. People may doubt or criticize your story, whether you're narrating a fictional story, pitching a business idea, or sharing a personal experience. Effectively responding to doubt necessitates combining affinity, evidence, and originality.

How to Overcome the Challenge of Objections and Skepticism

a. Be Original: Stories that seem authentic will elicit a stronger emotional response from readers. When discussing a personal experience, be open and truthful about your feelings and viewpoints. Being genuine fosters trust and facilitates audience connection-making.

b. Provide proof: You can increase the credibility of your story by providing proof to support it. Including supporting data, such as figures, testimonies, or professional opinions, will assist to alleviate concerns and address any issues.

c. Expect and Handle Objections: Consider potential objections before sharing your story. Incorporate anticipatory answers into your story to reduce any worries or skepticism that your audience may have. Proactively responding to criticism shows vision and faith in your story.

2. Cultural Sensitivities

Effective storytelling in a multicultural and interconnected society requires an awareness of and respect for cultural sensitivities. It takes considerable thought to navigate cultural differences so that your message is understood and treated with respect.

How to Overcome the Challenge of Cultural Sensitivities

a. Study Your Audience: Learn about the cultural practices of your target audience before you start writing your story. Recognize their cultural taboos, values, and beliefs. With this understanding, you may adapt your story to be sensitive to cultural differences and steer clear of unplanned pitfalls.

a. Accept Diversity: If your audience is heterogeneous, include that diversity in your narrative. Incorporate scenarios, people, or instances that illustrate different cultural viewpoints. A broader spectrum of people may relate to this inclusivity, which encourages a sense of belonging.

c. Request Feedback: If at all feasible, solicit feedback from people who come from different cultural backgrounds. They can offer insightful information and assist you in locating any potential blind spots. A varied set of advisors or beta readers can help create a story that is more inclusive and sensitive to cultural differences.

3. Modifying Your Story for Various Audiences

When it comes to narrative, one size does not fit all. Changing your tale to fit the distinct traits, inclinations, and expectations of other groups entails customizing your message.

How to Overcome the Challenge of Modifying Your Story for Various Audiences

a. Understand Your Audience: Good storytelling requires a thorough understanding of your audience. Take into account variables like prior knowledge, interests, age, and demographics. Tailoring your story to the tastes of your audience increases resonance and engagement.

b. Adjust Tone and Style: Your story's tone and style should appeal to the audience's sensibilities. Make your tale more approachable and engaging by modifying your vocabulary, tempo, and style, regardless of whether you're talking to a group of kids or a formal corporate audience.

c. Emphasize Relevant Themes: Various themes may speak to diverse audiences. Make sure the parts of your tale that are most likely to be relevant and engaging to your target audience are highlighted. This could entail changing the main idea, the cast of characters, or the setting to suit their preferences and issues.

Finally, storytelling is a flexible and influential art form. By addressing skepticism, managing cultural sensitivities, and tailoring your story to suit various audiences, you may improve your capacity to establish a lasting impression with your storytelling and connect with a wide range of people.

CHAPTER EIGHT

Assessing and Evaluating Storytelling Performance

Strong narrative techniques are essential for capturing attention, making points, and promoting relationships. However since the effects of a story can vary greatly, it's critical to use quantifiable measurements to gauge effectiveness. This chapter will examine the essential elements of gauging and assessing the effectiveness of storytelling, such as the application of Key Performance Indicators, the collection and evaluation of client input, and the significance of iterative storytelling improvement.

Storytelling's Key Performance Indicators (KPIs)

1. Metrics for Audience Engagement:

a. Duration of Engagement: Calculate how long viewers typically spend interacting with your story. Extended periods of involvement typically signify a more interesting story.

b. Rebound Rate: A reduced rebound rate shows that you were successful in holding the audience's attention with your tale.

2. Metrics for Social Media Engagement:

a. Shares and Retweets: These indicators show how well your story connects with readers and persuades them to tell their networks about it.

b. Comments and Responses: Examine the discussions your tale sparks to determine how well it resonates with readers.

3. Rates of Conversion:

a. Click-through Rates (CTRs): Track the proportion of visitors to your content that click on a call-to-action (CTA).

b. Conversion Rate: Determine how many sign-ups, purchases, or other desired activities resulted from your storytelling efforts.

4. Perception of Brands:

a. Brand Sentiment: After your narrative has been shared, use sentiment analysis tools to gauge how the audience feels about your brand.

b. Brand Recollection: Assess the extent to which your narrative aids in the recognition and recollection of your brand.

5. Analytics of Content Consumption:

a. Pageviews and Uncommon Visitors: Recognize the quantity and frequency of people who see your story.

b. Navigation Paths: Examine how users navigate your material to find interesting passages and possible places for them to lose interest.

Obtaining and Examining Client Feedback

1. Questionnaires and Surveys:

a. Post-narrative Surveys: After your narrative is presented to the audience, get responses right away to get a sense of how they are feeling.

b. Long-term Impact Surveys: Perform follow-up surveys to evaluate how your tale has affected people's perceptions and behaviors over time.

2. Listening on Social Media:

a. Monitor Mentions: Keep a record of any mentions of your content on social media and assess user attitude.

b. Hashtag tracking: Monitor the use of particular hashtags related to your storytelling effort, if applicable.

3. Focus Groups and Interviews: Hold focus groups or personalized interviews to learn more about the thoughts and feelings that your tale arouses in the audience.

4. Analysis of User-Generated Content (UGC): If your storytelling incorporates user input, examine user-generated content to comprehend users' perspectives and input.

Iterative Enhancement in Narration

1. A/B Comparisons:

a. Story Variations: Experiment with several iterations of your narrative to find components that connect with the audience more strongly.

b. CTA Experimentation: To maximize conversion rates, test out various calls to action.

2. Insights powered by analytics:

a. Iterative Analysis: To find opportunities for improvement, examine client feedback and performance indicators on a regular basis.

b. Content Evolution: Make use of findings to modify your narrative approach over time in order to maintain audience resonance and relevance.

3. Cooperative Education:

a. Cross-functional Collaboration: To obtain a variety of viewpoints and ideas, involve multiple teams such as marketing, content development, and data analytics.

b. Knowledge Sharing: To promote a culture of ceaseless development, it's important to disseminate learning throughout the company.

4. Trend Adjustment:

a. Stay Current: Stay up to speed on audience preferences, industry trends, and new storytelling forms so you can modify your strategy as needed.

b. Technology Integration: Adopt cutting-edge tools that can improve storytelling and audience participation.

In conclusion, a blend of qualitative and quantitative techniques is needed to measure and analyze the effectiveness of storytelling. Storytellers can evaluate their existing efforts and develop their narratives over time for greater effect by utilizing KPIs, getting customer feedback, and adopting iterative improvement.

CHAPTER NINE

Effective Storytelling in Sales

Effective storytelling has become a potent tool in the ever-changing world of sales, helping to engage consumers, foster relationships, and eventually increase revenue. This chapter explores the art of sales storytelling by looking at actual cases, taking notes from notable accomplishments, and offering advice on how to modify tactics for your company.

The Force of Storytelling in Sales

By appealing to emotions, storytelling builds a bond between the vendor and the customer. By leveraging the core elements of the human experience, successful sales tales increase the relatability of the good or service.

The cornerstone of any profitable sale is trust. Real-world tales demonstrate transparency, genuineness, and the beneficial effects of a good or service on past clients, all of which contribute to the development of trust.

Analyzing Actual Examples

1. The "Just Do It" Campaign by Nike

Nike's renowned "Just Do It" advertising campaign is a storytelling masterwork. The company offered athletic apparel in addition to giving its clients a sense of empowerment and resolve by showcasing genuine athletes conquering obstacles.

2. Success Stories on Salesforce

Customer relationship management (CRM) leader Salesforce highlights the observable advantages of their technology through success stories. The business successfully illustrates the worth of its product by showcasing actual companies that have prospered using Salesforce.

Two Crucial Takeaways From Famous Success Stories

1. Determine Who Your Audience Is

Stories that are successful are crafted to appeal to a certain target audience. Writing engaging tales requires a thorough awareness of your audience's requirements and goals, whether it is B2B or B2C.

2. Emphasizing Problems and Their Fixes

Relatable tales frequently center on a framework of problems and solutions. Determine the problems that your clients are facing and show them how your goods or services may help. This strategy increases the story's impact and relatability.

Three Approaches to Implement for Your Company

1. Recognize your USP or unique selling proposition.

Understanding your USP clearly is the first step in creating an engaging sales story. What unique qualities does your offering have? Make a lasting impression on your audience by conveying this uniqueness via your tale.

2. Make Use of Several Channels

Expand the reach of your story by using a variety of media. Expanding your storytelling platforms to include video material, blogs, social media, and traditional advertising will guarantee a larger audience and more interaction.

3. Promote Content Created by Users

Include success stories and client testimonials in your story. Because users may connect with each other's experiences, user-generated material lends authenticity and trustworthiness.

Ultimately, developing the skill of telling engaging tales can be revolutionary in the highly competitive field of sales. Convincing stories that connect with your audience requires careful consideration of practical examples, gaining knowledge from successful cases, and tailoring tactics to your industry. Using storytelling effectively can help you create enduring relationships, earn people's confidence, and launch profitable marketing efforts.

CHAPTER TEN

The Future of Sales Storytelling

Storytelling has become a potent weapon in the ever-changing sales market for engaging clients, fostering relationships, and increasing conversions. The future of sales storytelling is expected to be affected by new trends and technological advancements. In order to remain competitive in this ever-changing industry, one must be aware of these changes and take the initiative to implement new tactics.

Eight Ways that Storytelling Can Be Relevant in the Future

1. The Emergence of Immersive Technologies: Technologies such as augmented and virtual reality (VR/AR) are becoming more and more essential to the sales process. Imagine taking a prospective customer to a virtual showroom where they may interact with items in a realistic setting. Storytelling is improved by this immersive experience since it fosters meaningful and lasting relationships. It is imperative for sales professionals to include these technologies in their storytelling, offering a multi-sensory encounter that surpasses conventional PowerPoint presentations.

2. Tailored Interactive Content: Interactive and tailored storytelling is the way of the future in sales. Sales teams will be able to examine enormous volumes of data owing to the emergence of artificial intelligence (AI) and machine learning, which will let them customize their stories to each customer's tastes. Customers will be more deeply engaged with interactive information, including dynamic presentations or personalized movies, which will also help them feel more understood and connected.

3. Selling with stories on Social Media: Social media sites are still quite important in influencing how people behave. The key to the future of sales storytelling is making the most of these venues to connect with more people. Salespeople will need to become experts at selling with stories, which involves creating captivating tales to draw in prospects on websites like LinkedIn, Instagram, and TikTok.

4. Integration of Conversational AI and Chatbots: As AI-powered chatbots advance in sophistication, they will become indispensable in the storytelling process. Envision a sales assistant who can guide clients through a customized sales experience in a conversational and organic manner. Salespeople need to know how to smoothly include conversational AI into their storytelling procedures so that it can offer insightful data and support instantly.

5. Data-Driven Storytelling: The landscape of sales will keep changing as a result of data analytics. Salespeople will create stories that connect with their intended audience by utilizing data-driven insights. Developing tales that specifically address requirements and difficulties will require an understanding of customer habits, choices, and pain areas.

6. The Evolution of Story Metrics: In the future, sales storytelling will be evaluated using sophisticated metrics, just like in traditional marketing. In addition to conversion rates, sales teams will evaluate consumer feedback, time spent on content, and engagement levels in order to continuously improve their storylines. More potent story techniques and iterative adjustments will be possible with this data-driven approach.

7. Human-Centric Storytelling in a Tech-Driven World: Although technology will certainly influence sales storytelling in the future, the importance of the human aspect cannot be overstated. Realism, compassion, and emotional ties will always be essential elements of compelling stories. To make sure their tales connect with customers on a personal level, salespeople need to strike a balance between using technology and taking a human-centered approach.

8. Ceaseless Acquisition of Knowledge: A ceaseless acquisition of Knowledge is necessary to be relevant in the ever-changing sales industry. Salespeople need to put in the effort to learn about new consumer trends, technological advancements, and the changing storytelling landscape. To thrive in a continuously changing world, one must be adaptable through the acquisition of knowledge.

In summary, the field of sales storytelling has a bright future ahead of it owing to the shifting consumer expectations and technology breakthroughs. In a progressive and competitive market, those who embrace these developments and integrate immersive technologies, personalized content, and data-driven insights into their sales story will establish themselves as leaders. The secret is realizing that storytelling is a progressive process that changes with the times and necessitates a dedication to creativity and constant growth, not merely a tool.

CONCLUSION

Finally, 'Master the Art of Storytelling to Sell Like Crazy' is an all-inclusive manual for anyone looking to use the power of captivating storytelling to boost their skill of salesmanship. We've covered the fundamentals of storytelling on these pages, looking at how to tell stories that capture, connect, and eventually persuade. Through an appreciation of the psychology of narrative and its tremendous effects on human emotions, readers have acquired relevant knowledge about connecting with their audience and leaving a lasting impression.

The significance of originality in storytelling has been asserted in this book, which encourages readers to incorporate their own experiences and sincere emotions into their stories. It transcends traditional sales tactics by demonstrating how a compelling story can dissolve barriers, build rapport, and make a potential buyer feel relatable. With our exploration of a variety of storytelling approaches, from developing captivating characters to skillfully organizing narratives, readers now possess the useful tools necessary to bring their stories to life and leave a lasting impression on their intended audience.

A strong difference in the fast-paced, cutthroat world of sales is the capacity to create engaging stories. In addition to offering the required techniques and resources, 'Master the Art of Storytelling to Sell Like Crazy' encourages readers to adopt a different perspective by viewing sales as chances to engage and connect with people more deeply rather than as transactions.

As you set out to become an expert at telling stories, keep in mind that the real magic is found in the sincere and real connections you make with your stories. If you're a newbie to entrepreneurship or an experienced sales expert, the insights in this book will definitely help you change the way you approach sales. So, go forward with confidence, let your inner storyteller loose, and observe as your uncanny ability to sell turns into a formidable force in the business world.